BERNIE SANDERS
THE ESSENTIAL GUIDE

SQUINT

BRIEF BOOKS FOR A BUSY WORLD
Look More Closely

BERNIE SANDERS

THE ESSENTIAL GUIDE

OKLA ELLIOTT

 **EYEWEAR** PUBLISHING

First published in 2016
by Eyewear Publishing Ltd
Suite 38, 19-21 Crawford Street
Marylebone, London W1H 1PJ
United Kingdom

Typeset with graphic design by Edwin Smet
Author photo by Robert MacCready
Printed in England by TJ International Ltd, Padstow, Cornwall

The right of Okla Elliott to be identified as author of
this work has been asserted in accordance with section 77
of the Copyright, Designs and Patents Act 1988

ISBN 978-1-908998-94-1

Eyewear wishes to thank Jonathan Wonham for his very generous patronage of our press.

The editor has generally followed American spelling and punctuation at the author's request.

WWW.EYEWEARPUBLISHING.COM

CONTENTS

THE BERNIE SANDERS TIMELINE

1941: Sanders is born in Brooklyn, New York

1962: Sanders leads a weeks-long civil rights sit-in in Chicago

1981: Sanders wins mayoral race in Burlington, Vermont

1983: Sanders is re-elected as mayor with a 21-point win

1984: Sanders creates the first municipal housing land trust in the nation, which has become a worldwide model for affordable housing

1990: Sanders is elected to his first of eight terms in the U.S. House of Representatives

1993: Sanders votes against NAFTA

1996: Sanders votes against the Defense of Marriage Act

2001: Sanders votes against the U.S. Patriot Act

2002: Sanders votes against the Iraq War

2006: Sanders is elected to the U.S. Senate

2015: Sanders enters the Democratic race for president

A SOMEWHAT PERSONAL PREFACE

"There are millions and millions of people who are tired of establishment politics, who are tired of corporate greed, who want a candidate that will help lead a mass movement in this country [...] What people are saying is, 'Enough is enough. The billionaire class cannot have it all.'" – Bernie Sanders[1]

The purpose of this book is to introduce readers to Bernie Sanders, his ideas, and his campaign. It is also intended to put Sanders and his enthusiastic movement into global, historical, and philosophical context. Therefore, it includes elements of biography, campaign coverage, historical analysis, political philosophy, and social commentary. I certainly hope this short book will help Sanders win the Democratic nomination and be elected president of the United States, but I also hope it will help explain how his phenomenal popularity came about and how we might best utilize this enthusiasm throughout the campaign season and beyond.

Like many people, I first encountered the name Bernie Sanders via viral internet memes over the years – photos of the senator with his arm outstretched, a finger punctuating the air rhetorically, an incisive quote floating beside his image. I "liked" and shared these memes as did so many millions of progressives around the United States and the world. When progressive groups began draft petitions to get Sanders into the presidential race, pundits wrote the effort off as a leftist fantasy. Hillary Clinton was inevitable, we were told, and many of us believed it.

But then something happened that no one had foreseen: Sanders entered the race and immediately began drawing the largest crowds of any candidate in either major party. And shortly thereafter, he began drawing the largest crowds in U.S. primary history. It all seemed organic and inexplicable, but I will argue that it was Sanders – and more importantly his movement – that were inevitable at this moment in history, not Hillary Clinton. I will argue that his candidacy is an outgrowth of movements like Occupy Wall Street and others, and that they themselves in turn were outgrowths of dissatisfaction with the neoliberal and neoconservative revolutions of the 1990s and early 2000s. Sanders is the focused tip of a long historical spear, and he is our best weapon against politics-as-usual and the ruinous economic, environmental, and diplomatic factors at play in the world today. If you want to understand his policy positions and how we can continue to grow this important movement, I invite you to follow me here on my exploration of Sanders's rise to prominence.

But first allow me to add a quick personal note, so that you know a bit more about where I'm coming from. I will try to be as intellectually honest and objective as possible in these pages, but perfect objectivity falls outside the realm of mortal possibility, and in this case it is not even the goal. I am an avid Sanders supporter, as will become obvious, if it isn't already, and I came to this position largely by way of studying the facts as closely as I could. I say *largely* because I came to this position due to certain personal and emotional reasons as well.

Neither of my parents graduated high school; today I have a PhD and am a professor and writer, a career path my parents never dreamed possible for me and that would have been utterly unthinkable without public education. I could perhaps claim to have *pulled myself up by my bootstraps*. I would like us, however, to ditch that most disingenuous of notions. (The phrase itself began as an expression of impossibility, in fact.) I went to public schools and public universities for my entire education. Public school was of course free, and I might be a member of the last generation of working-class college graduates who didn't graduate with crushing debt. This background is one of the many reasons I support Bernie Sanders and his movement.

I hope by the end of this book, you will be a supporter as well. Or as the internet would have it: I hope you will be #feelingtheBern.

WHO IS BERNIE SANDERS?

"My father came to this country from Poland without a penny in his pocket and without much of an education. My mother graduated high school in New York City. My father worked for almost his entire life as a paint salesman and we were solidly lower-middle class. My parents, brother and I lived in a small rent-controlled apartment. My mother's dream was to move out of that small apartment into a home of our own. She died young and her dream was never fulfilled. As a kid I learned, in many, many ways, what lack of money means to a family. That's a lesson I have never forgotten." – Bernie Sanders[2]

Bernie Sanders appears to have little interest in talking about himself. Aside from a few interviews in which he has been basically forced to answer personal questions and one rally during which he hugged a Muslim student and mentioned his Jewish background to show solidarity with the bigotry she had experienced, Sanders sticks to the issues confronting Americans instead of playing the political soap-opera game so many politicians engage in. I will therefore follow his lead and keep this section brief. That said, however, people are curious about Bernie Sanders the man, and I believe his background and family life have influenced his policies in a variety of ways. It is therefore important to offer a sketch of the salient facts about Sanders's personal life for voters to consider.

Sanders was born in on September 8, 1941, in Brooklyn, New York. His father was a Polish-Jewish immigrant whose family died in the Holocaust, and the family lived in rent-controlled housing for many years. He attended the Brooklyn College for a year before transferring to the University of Chicago, where he received his BA in political science. While there, Sanders famously participated in the first civil rights sit-in in Chicago history.

Sanders has said that his early family experiences and college years have affected him deeply. Hearing about the Holocaust at a young age impressed upon Sanders the horrors that can occur if people do not take a political stand against demagoguery, and seeing the way housing policies affected him and his working-class family, he realized that compassionate and fair-minded government policies can prove a positive force in the lives of Americans. Being on the frontlines of the Civil Rights Movement of 1960s engrained in him an understanding of racial and economic oppression and how to combat it.

Those are the broad strokes of Sanders's life, but what about the daily details? Sanders is precisely what you would expect. He recently confessed that he has never worn a tuxedo, his suits are not expensively tailored, and his now-famous hair is as independent as the man himself. According to a recent *People* magazine article, he does his own laundry and own grocery shopping unlike many senators, lives in a modest home, and leads a minimalist lifestyle in general. In that same article, his wife joked that if he owned seven sweaters, that would three too many.[3]

Sanders's wife, Jane O'Meara Sanders, grew up Catholic and working class. Here is a snapshot of her educational and professional career:

> As a young mother, Jane worked as a bank teller and a supermarket cashier, and she demonstrated against the war in Vietnam [...] At Vermont's Goddard College, Jane finished her undergraduate degree, in social work. She took a job at the Burlington Police Department, in the Juvenile Division, then as a community organizer at the King Street Area Youth Center. And she helped pay off student loans as a VISTA

volunteer [...] In the 1980s, Jane helped start a newspaper, a teen center, after-school programs, and a day care. [4] Given their working-class backgrounds, Sanders and his wife both equally understand the plight of the average American, and they have both dedicated their lives to improving the lives of others.

Jane Sanders has three children from a previous marriage and four grandchildren. Sanders has one biological son, Levi Sanders, who lives in New Hampshire and "currently works as a social security disability insurance senior analyst at Boston-based Cambridge & Somerville Legal Services, handling insurance claims in disability cases for both children and adults." [5] Levi has three children adopted from China. Sanders has cited his grandchildren – his son's three adopted children and his wife's four biological grandchildren – as a driving force in his thinking about the future of our country and the world at large.

In the final analysis, Sanders has a large and diverse family (about which, more later) and one that has had various degrees of influence on his political thinking. Now that you know a bit more about the man, let's discuss his movement.

A HISTORIC MOVEMENT
(VIEWED HISTORICALLY)

"Economic powers continue to justify the current global system where priority tends to be given to speculation and the pursuit of financial gain, which fail to take the context into account, let alone the effects on human dignity and the natural environment. Here we see how environmental deterioration and human and ethical degradation are closely linked."
– Pope Francis[6]

The Sanders campaign has proven historic in several ways. Sanders has received more individual donations than has any primary candidate in history, and these donations are all small-dollar donations averaging around $30 each. He also has eschewed billionaires' donations, yet he has kept up with Clinton's fundraising and beaten all of the Republicans' by significant margins. The crowd sizes at his rallies are likewise historic, breaking all previous records. This level of political enthusiasm is unprecedented, eclipsing even that enjoyed by Barack Obama in the 2007-2008 primary cycle.

We have to take a historical view of this historic campaign in order to understand where all of this intense enthusiasm for Sanders and his candidacy is coming from. Like most phenomena, the Bernie Sanders movement was not born fully grown, but rather has a series of precursors. I argue that the Wisconsin protests of 2011, and the Occupy movement which emerged concurrently with those protests, set the stage to make the Sanders movement possible. Without that bedrock of progressive activism, there wouldn't have been a sufficiently solid foundation upon which to build the Sanders movement. But there were likewise economic and political conditions that gave rise to these foundation-building movements. The neoliberal and neoconservative revolutions of the 1990s and early 2000s demanded a leftist-populist response of equal proportions, and just as those damaging revolutions in economic and foreign policy worked on a global scale, I argue that the leftist-populist response is likewise global in nature, though perhaps more organic and less organized.

Politics and its principles do not enjoy the elegant and abstract perfection that physical laws in the hard sciences possess. Even the mathematical aspects of the social sciences – that is to say, statistics – are already married to the messy process of polling and are subject to the most radical of reversals. That said, however, there are discernible forces at play, and discernible patterns of human behavior. The rise of political figures such as Elizabeth Warren in the United States, Jeremy Corbyn in the United Kingdom, Justin Trudeau in Canada, José Mujica in Uruguay, and Evo Morales in Bolivia in recent years shows a growing unrest in the system as it currently stands. Recent elections around the world are likewise telling of a global shift away from austerity and capitalism-über-alles policies.

Perhaps the figure Sanders most resembles is Jeremy Corbyn in Britain. As the BBC writes:

> The comparisons are irresistible. They are both silver-haired socialists who rail against inequality and the political establishment – and make the style police despair. Few outside of politics had heard of them this time last year. Both men were reluctant to enter their respective contests and did not think they stood a chance of winning. [7]

And here in the United States, the *Wall Street Journal* has made a similar comparison:

> Like Bernie Sanders in the Democratic presidential race, Mr. Corbyn has electrified disenchanted young voters, leading to a surge in support for his

antiquated brand of socialism. New members have flocked to join the party, while his rallies overflow with fans enthralled by his "authenticity."[8]

There are of course differences between Corbyn and Sanders, foremost among them the fact that Sanders is more moderate and pragmatic in certain respects, but the similarities are hard to miss.

What is fascinating is that without any apparent coordination between the aforementioned leaders, their response to neoliberal and neoconservative policies is remarkably synchronized. If we took twenty quotes from each of these leaders without attribution, even their most diehard followers would be hard-pressed to identify who said each one, as their messages are so similar.

And the move toward various kinds of democratic socialist thought is not limited to the political arena. Senator Sanders and Pope Francis have much in common in their ethical and political visions, and both enjoy a large popularity among the Left. I want to be as clear as possible here: it would be utterly wrong-minded to view all of this as mere coincidence. There are subterranean cultural, economic, political, and even psychological forces at play, bringing these leaders and their message to the fore at this point in history.

As many commentators have found opportunity to observe, this election cycle has been in many ways a referendum on politics as usual and on the establishment. If we take Donald Trump and Ben Carson on the Republican side, their narratives have been largely ones of independence from establishment control and outsider authenticity. Trump in particular taps into the anger many Americans feel when they see their wages stagnating even though they are working longer hours, when they are driven into bankruptcy due to medical bills, or when they can't afford to send their children to college. In effect, Trump agrees with Sanders that these are all problems that Americans face today; he simply differs on the solutions, and radically. His rhetoric scapegoats Muslims and Mexican immigrants and his policies cut taxes for the rich, and employ other such classic rightwing measures.

All that said, however, I don't want to neatly equate the right-wing populism we see among Trump supporters and the left-wing populism among Sanders supporters. As Norman Solomon writes:

> Elite media often blur distinctions
> between right-wing populism and

progressive populism – as though there's
not all that much difference between
appealing to xenophobia and racism on
the one hand and appealing for social
justice and humanistic solidarity on the
other. [9]

Solomon's distinctions here are accurate and
important, but I still maintain that the same
underlying economic and social problems have
given rise to these two populist responses.
The same conditions created these opposing
enthusiasms.

Enthusiasm itself has become a major topic
of conversation during this election cycle, with
Sanders hosting massive rallies while Clinton
has drawn anemic crowds, with Trump bragging
almost daily about his huge support base and Bush
lagging badly in terms of voter enthusiasm. I want
us to take a longer philosophical view of political
enthusiasm.

Sidney Axinn discusses German
philosopher Immanuel Kant's views on the French
Revolution in the following terms: "In Kant's
philosophy of history, crisis or tension is necessary
for human progress."[10] As Axinn suggests, Kant's
theory of human progress requires that a crisis or
tension exists for things to move forward, because

these crises awaken the political consciousness of the people. We have certainly had an abundance of crises and tensions over the past decade, but the actual roots of the Bernie Sanders Revolution go even further back, to the neoliberal and neoconservative reforms of late twentieth and early twenty-first centuries that ushered in massive international trade agreements, weakened unions, corporatized universities, and perpetual war in the Middle East. These were the political moves that led to the tensions and crises we currently face and for which the Sanders movement is the solution, in large part because his movement has the commitment and enthusiasm to see the struggle through to the end.

Immanuel Kant looked at the French Revolution itself – that is, the actual historical events of the French Revolution – as largely a failure, but he considered the French Revolution a grand and important event for the progress of humanity toward more humane laws, more equal and fair distribution of wealth, and a point of inspiration for those who would see humanity better its station. How could he hold what seem at first glance to be contradictory notions of this single (and singular) event? It centered on what he called *enthusiasm* and his belief that the revitalization of enthusiasm for human dignity and the struggle for a more equitable and rational society was more important than a single success or failure along the way to achieving these goals. I cannot get on board with Kant's view that history is inexorably moving toward a better and more rational future, but I do think that we can move it in that direction, if only for a time.

It is also worth briefly mentioning the German word for enthusiasm – *Begeisterung* – contains the root word *Geist*, which means *mind* or *spirit*. I mention this only because it is a mindful and spirited enthusiasm we need, not a blind one. And here I want to point out one aspect the Bernie Sanders campaign that is largely overlooked: Sanders is an educator. Much of his stump speech is laden with statistics, names of congressional bills, and facts that likely feel obscure to the majority of the American people. How many had even heard of "Glass-Steagall" before this election cycle? How many understand how super PACs work, legally speaking? And when it comes to that most convoluted of subjects, healthcare, the micro- and macro-economics of the issue can be baffling.

Once the American people more fully understand these issues, they will realize that we need substantive change in nearly every area of our society. This is especially important in terms of the Democratic primary, because despite what we typically imagine, Democrats are generally less interested in candidates for change and more conservative in the sense of supporting candidates who are perceived as safe, in this election cycle especially:

> Since March, the share of all registered voters who say it is more important for a presidential candidate to have "new ideas and a different approach" has surged – with virtually all of the increase coming among Republican and Republican-leaning voters. Today, by more than two-to-one (65 percent to 29 percent), Republican and Republican-leaning registered voters say it is more important that a candidate have new ideas than "experience and a proven record." Opinion among Democratic voters continues to be more evenly divided: 50 percent say it is more important for a candidate to have experience and a proven record, while 42 percent view new ideas and a different approach as more important. This is little changed from March (46 percent

experience, 49 percent new ideas).[11] This phenomenon, I think, is indicative of a larger issue among Democrats. Republicans tend to support the candidates they actually support, whereas Democrats want to find a moderate that can appease a wider swath of voters.

At first glance, this approach can seem like a wise move, but let's think about those times in recent history when Democrats chose the safe, moderate (and let's be honest, *boring*) candidate and how it worked out. Though Al Gore's candidacy had all of the well-known issues in Florida, he was not a candidate to rile up the base. He even lost his own state. His flat demeanor and calculatedly safe policy positions bored the Democratic base and gave rise to a more exciting candidacy by Ralph Nader. Whatever one's opinion of Nader, it is undeniable that he brought in first-time voters in a way Gore's safeness never did. And then we had John Kerry, another safe establishment politician who bored the Democratic base. People voted for Kerry largely as an anything-but-Bush measure, and that is no way to win elections.

Now the establishment of the Democratic Party is suggesting another middle-of-the-road candidate, only this time the candidate is also among the most hated figures in Republican circles. Clinton will therefore bore the Democratic base while riling up the Republican base, regardless of who becomes the Republican candidate. She is therefore doubly bad, in terms of enthusiasm and negative enthusiasm. Clinton is not the right leader for this moment in history, when we need real change and have ample enthusiasm to achieve it.

Just recall what happened when we nominated Barack Obama, who was not considered a moderate yet who riled the Democratic base. We won by a massive margin. Sanders creates similar if not greater enthusiasm, if his rallies and number of donations are meaningful indicators, and he has the added strength of bringing in millions of previously unengaged citizens from across the entire cultural spectrum.

I want to pause now to make a strong appeal to liberals and leftists to resist the urge to look down on Trump supporters and others like them. Condescension is perhaps the worst of all rhetorical tactics. Telling people they are stupid or racist or xenophobic will not convince them of our position and will not turn them into Sanders supporters. We must find common ground with our fellow citizens, no matter how wide the gulf seems between us and them. What Sanders – and we, his supporters – have to do is convince these people that they're right to be angry that their standard of living is in decline and that their futures don't look as bright as they once did. We have turn their negative enthusiasm, which is too often aimed at scapegoating or comprised of ideologically damaging beliefs, into a positive enthusiasm for Sanders, whose policies will actually improve their lives. They are a part of this moment in history, and their concerns are very real, as will be the consequences of their votes in the primaries and the general election.

Another way Sanders is an outgrowth of this particular moment in history is his dominance of social media. Much of the support for various mass movements or single concerns foment in the cyber-spacial fields of social media. For example, the #BlackLivesMatter movement is generally written as I have it here, with a hashtag as part of the name itself, and the Occupy movement thrived in large part due to social media. The majority of Sanders's support has come in the form of social media activism, and given the disproportionate coverage other candidates like Trump and Clinton have received during the primaries – with Trump receiving twenty-one times as much coverage according to one study – the Sanders campaign would have died on the vine without the nourishment of his social media advocates.[12]

There are many vocal critics of social media, and I share some of their concerns, but in terms of its potential for democratic action, it must be seen as a net positive. The aforementioned Occupy movement, for example, first broke into the mainstream media by journalists covering not the movement itself but the social media phenomenon it created. And, here again, there could have been no Occupy movement as we understand it without the powers and reach of social media.

Let's move now to perhaps the largest obstacle Sanders faces: his self-identification as a democratic socialist. The term *democratic socialism* is in decline as a hated term, but many still misunderstand it.

WHAT DOES *DEMOCRATIC SOCIALISM* MEAN, AND SHOULD WE SUPPORT IT?

"And, by the way, almost everything [FDR] proposed was called 'socialist'. Social Security, which transformed life for the elderly in this country was 'socialist'. The concept of the 'minimum wage' was seen as a radical intrusion into the marketplace and was described as 'socialist'. Unemployment insurance, abolishing child labor, the 40-hour work week, collective bargaining, strong banking regulations, deposit insurance, and job programs that put millions of people to work were all described, in one way or another, as 'socialist'. Yet, these programs have become the fabric of our nation and the foundation of the middle class." – Bernie Sanders[13]

We live in a time when the sixty-two richest people own more wealth than the bottom 350 million people. Take a moment and really let that idea take full root in your mind. Sixty-two people own more wealth than 350 million people do. That appalling fact itself, however, would not have been enough to give rise to these progressive movements. There had to be a corollary shift in attitudes about this state of affairs. It is therefore worth noting that Americans' attitudes toward socialism have improved drastically in recent years, a fact especially true among those under thirty-five years old. According poll after poll, the term "socialism" is becoming less scary and more positive, but what is even more striking is that the policies of democratic socialism have overwhelming support among Americans. A Gallup poll from 2015 shows that "52 percent support a redistribution of wealth through heavily taxing the rich, for example – the highest number that Gallup has seen since first asking that question in 1940. And 63 percent of Americans believe that the current distribution of wealth in the U.S. is unfair." [14]

There is some debate as to whether Sanders is indeed a democratic socialist, despite identifying as one. Many have claimed that he is in fact a social democrat. Splitting hairs over terminology might seem like an academic exercise with little or no value, and it largely is, but since Republicans like Rand Paul and Donald Trump – as well as Clinton surrogates – have tried to equate Sanders with dictatorial communist leaders like Stalin, we have to concede that terminology matters. Perhaps more important is that the American public generally doesn't fully understand the distinctions between communism, various kinds of socialism, or social programs. Since the term *democratic socialism* isn't likely to go away, and Sanders isn't likely to stop identifying with the concept, we need not only to define what he means by it but defend what he means by it. Here is how he defined the term himself in 2006:

> Well, I think it means the government has got to play a very important role in making sure that as a right of citizenship, all of our people have healthcare; that as a right, all of our kids, regardless of income, have quality childcare, are able to go to college without going deeply into debt; that it means we do not allow large corporations and moneyed interests to destroy our environment; that we create a government in which it is not dominated by big money interest. I mean, to me, it means democracy, frankly. That's all it means. [15]

These are all political objectives that the majority of Americans agree with, but it is essential that we win the public debate that these are the goals we should pursue, and we must counter the mendacious attacks on what Sanders stands for.

We live in what's called *a mixed economy* – that is, we have capitalist enterprises existing alongside socialist programs like police departments, fire departments, snowplow services, public schools, public roads, Medicare and Medicaid, and the military. The real debate is not whether we want some socialism in our economy, it's where and how much. What Sanders means by *democratic socialism* is a mixed economy that offers more robust social programs such as universal healthcare, free college tuition, increased Social Security benefits, and greater investment in services like public transportation. He does not mean the centralized control of the economy or nationalization of natural resources, as some of his critics have claimed. In effect, he would like to implement an economy more like those found in Western Europe, where capitalism is alive and well, but people aren't strapped with $100,000 in student debt and aren't ruined financially by a single medical emergency.

One common bit of misinformation is that countries like Canada or Denmark or Germany are so saddled with taxes to pay for these more robust social programs that there is little or no room for social mobility. According to the right-of-center publication *The Economist*, this is not actually true:

> The study, by a clutch of economists at Harvard University and the University of California, Berkeley, is far bigger than

any previous effort to measure social mobility. The economists crunch numbers from over 40m tax returns of people born between 1971 and 1993 (with all identifying information removed). They focus on mobility between generations and use several ways to measure it, including the correlation of parents' and children's income, and the odds that a child born into the bottom fifth of the income distribution will climb all the way up to the top fifth.

This is therefore the largest and most thorough study of its kind, conducted at two of the greatest research institutions on the planet. And what did they find?

They find that none of these measures has changed much. In 1971 a child from the poorest fifth had an 8.4 percent chance of making it to the top quintile. For a child born in 1986 the odds were 9 percent. The study confirms previous findings that America's social mobility is low compared with many European countries. (In Denmark, a poor child has twice as much chance of making it to the top quintile as in America.) [16]

It is not just abundantly clear that democratic socialism of the Sanders variety can work, but also that it works better than the system we currently have in the United States in terms of social mobility. This finding is key, since part of the right-wing mythology is that democratic socialism fetters people so much that they have no chance of improving their social standing through hard work, when in fact it is the opposite.

And why might this be the case? The answer is simple if we think about it properly. What is the primary means of improving one's station in life? Education is consistently cited as the number-one factor in this arena, so when education is either entirely or largely free, poor citizens can afford to attend universities and trade schools, thus acquiring the skills needed to climb higher in society without also acquiring stifling amounts of debt.

But Americans likely need more convincing. Many people only hear *tax increase* when someone says *democratic socialism*. They don't realize how much the vast super-majority of us would save if we had stronger social programs. Gerald Friedman, an economist at the University of Massachusetts at Amherst, predicts the following in terms of overall savings for the American people if we instate

Sanders's plan for healthcare:

> Sanders's Medicare-for-all plan would
> save $6 trillion over the next ten years
> compared with the current system,
> in large part by eliminating what
> the Sanders campaign described as
> "expensive and wasteful private health
> insurance." [17]

According to nearly every econometric measure out there, democratic socialism works for the majority of the population, and the myths of capitalism and neoliberalism are demonstrably false. I say *demonstrably false* because the facts about the issue point us to this conclusion. And facts are what Bernie Sanders is about.

The difference between neoconservative/neoliberal argumentation and the kinds of arguments Sanders puts forth is their relationship to reality. The former is largely characterized by ideological abstractions and anecdotal evidence; the latter is largely characterized by unadorned use of fact. We hear regularly from the right that money trickles down. This is utterly false. Money trickles up. Raise the minimum wage to $15 dollars an hour, as Sanders suggests we do incrementally over the next few years, and the average worker will have more dispensable income to buy anything from

Doritos to poetry books to gasoline. The producers of these products – essential or inessential as you might find any of them – end up with this worker's money. In effect, everyone wins. The worker gets the product and the producer gets the money. This is why we have seen, without a single exception, economic growth in those cities and states that have instated a higher minimum wage.

> New data released by the Department of Labor shows that raising the minimum wage does not appear to have had a negative impact on job growth, contrary to what critics said would happen. In a report on Friday, the 13 states that raised their minimum wages on Jan. 1 have added jobs at a faster pace than those that did not. [18]

It is not enough that the facts support Sanders in all of his policies; we must make sure that everyone knows these facts. The myth that raising the minimum wage will harm the economy is pervasive and persistent, and we must combat it with actual economic facts at every turn in order to convince voters that Sanders is right on this and on his other democratic socialist policies. And it is precisely these sorts of policies that can increase upward mobility in the Unites States, a place where we pride ourselves (rightly or wrongly) on all people having the opportunity to become anything they want.

Furthermore, even though the word *socialism* in any of its iterations is the equivalent of a curse word among some (though as previously mentioned, that attitude is changing rapidly), the ideas Sanders is putting forward are very much in the mainstream of Americans' beliefs. As Juan Cole writes:

> Some 63 percent of Americans agree that the current distribution of wealth is unfair. And in a Gallup poll done earlier this month, a majority, 52 percent, think that government taxation on the rich should be used to reduce the wealth gap. This percentage is historically high, having been only 45 percent in 1998. But there seems to be a shift going on, because Gallup got the 52 percent proportion in answer to the question on taxing the rich both in April and again in May of this year. [19]

All of these are key issues for the Sanders campaign, and the majority of people agree with him. And it doesn't stop there. Americans agree with Sanders at even higher rates on other key issues:

> Some 79 percent of Americans believe that education beyond high school is not affordable for everyone. And some 57 percent of people under 30 believe student debt is a problem for youth. [20]

And, finally:

> According to a very recent Yale/Gallup poll, some 71 percent of Americans believe global warming is occurring, and 57 percent are sure that human activity (emitting greenhouse gases like carbon dioxide) is causing it, while another 12 percent think the warming is at least partly human-caused. That's 69 percent who blame human beings wholly or in part. [21]

In effect, the American people agree with Sanders on all the major issues, even as some may have a misunderstanding of what *democratic socialism* actually entails. It is therefore incumbent upon his supporters to educate everyone around us on what Sanders means by *democratic socialism*. We will also have to educate people about his policy positions and voting record, since detractors in both the Democratic and Republican parties may attempt to distort these.

It is also my hope that Sanders makes further efforts to explain to voters what he stands for and why they shouldn't be scared of the term *democratic socialism*. Since he is one of the few candidates who listens to his supporters, perhaps we can nudge him in that direction with our own consistent attempts to explain these issues to the voting public.

SCIENCE FICTION AND THE ANXIETIES OF OUR CULTURE (A THEORETICAL INTERLUDE)

"We must, whether were like each other or not, work together. We have no choice in the matter." – Isaac Asimov[22]

Allow me a brief theoretical detour. I recently co-authored a longish science fiction novel, and in my day job as a literature professor, I teach a world literature class centered on science fiction from around the globe. One thing that regularly comes up in scholarship and popular discussions on science fiction is that it often dramatizes the anxieties of a culture. It has been often suggested, for example, that *Night of the Living Dead* (1968) expressed unconscious and conscious anxieties about the Cold War and communism. Let's look at recent science fiction movies and novels.

In *Automata* (2014), we see an ecological wasteland and a protagonist in a dead-end job at a soulless corporation who asks his pregnant wife whether it is wise to bring a child into this world. This film encapsulates several major anxieties afoot today: worry about the environment is at an all-time high, distrust of major corporations permeates the culture on both the left and the right, and people are concerned about their children's future given the skyrocketing tuition at colleges and the aforementioned environmental worry.

And let's look more generally at the tone of science fiction narratives in recent years. If you look back to the 1990s, most science fiction ended on a happy or uplifting note, even when some horrifying things occurred during the course of the story. Not so in recent years. Movies like *The Last Days on Mars* (2013) and *Europa Report* (2013) are unrelentingly bleak, ending with all of the major characters dead, leaving no real hope. It is worth noting that both of these films were released after the 2008 economic calamity, which ushered in a new era of despair for many.

Bernie Sanders's proposals are so popular among voters at this particular moment in history precisely because they answer these anxieties. Famed scientist and novelist Isaac Asimov said that we have to think science-fictionally if we are going to have any hope of saving our planet and our species. What he meant by this is that we have to have a bold vision for the future and we have to meld our imagination, scientific information, and political willpower to combat the issues facing us. Unlike any other candidate, Sanders does so:

What happens in Syria, for example [...]
When you have drought, when people
can't grow their crops, they're going to
migrate into cities and when people
migrate into cities and when they don't
have jobs, there's going to be a lot more
instability, a lot more unemployment
and people will be subject to the types
of propaganda that Al Qaeda and ISIS
are using right now and so where you
have discontent you have instability,
that's where problems arise and certainly
without a doubt, a climate change will
lead to that. [23]

This is precisely the kind of mix of science and
imagination and politics that Asimov meant
when he said we must think science-fictionally.
Sanders's ability to see the connections between
environmental issues and terrorism is the kind of
thinking that allowed him to foresee the regional
problems the Iraq War would cause (which we will
discuss in the chapter on foreign policy).

Interestingly, the Sanders campaign website
recently published an article by Bill McKibben
titled "The Night of the Living Dead, Climate
Change-Style." In this article, McKibben equates
certain political issues surrounding environmental

concerns as undead monsters that must be battled in what seems like a never-ending struggle to the kill the unkillable. As McKibben writes: "So many petitions, so many demonstrations, so many meetings. But at least for now, there's really no other way to kill a zombie."[24] I don't want to make too much of this obvious coincidence; I long ago developed this theory about science fiction and the anxieties of a culture, and I had written a draft of this section of the book before I saw the McKibben article; but I do think it's telling that these science-fictional metaphors should come up precisely at a time when our anxieties are running especially high, and I find it entirely appropriate that another writer in support of Sanders made use of such metaphors.

I thank you for your forbearance in allowing me to offer a pet theory about the role of science fiction in our culture; let's now move on to a more traditional discussion of these major issues facing us today and creating so many of these aforementioned anxieties. I have broken the issues down into campaign finance reform, criminal justice reform, economic policy, education policy, environmental policy, gun control, foreign policy, and identity politics, largely focusing on Sanders's record on each of these issues and how they fit into the current political discourse.

CAMPAIGN FINANCE REFORM

"The need for real campaign finance reform is not a progressive issue. It is not a conservative issue. It is an American issue. It is an issue that should concern all Americans, regardless of their political point of view, who wish to preserve the essence of the longest standing democracy in the world, a government that represents all of the people and not a handful of powerful and wealthy special interests."
– Bernie Sanders[25]

In 2010 the Supreme Court ruled by a five-to-four vote in the case *Citizens United v. Federal Election Commission* that entities such as corporations and unions could spend unlimited amounts of money on independent political expenditures. Bernie Sanders has repeatedly called this the most disastrous court decision in modern history and has promised that any nominee of his to the Supreme Court would have to be willing to overturn the decision. Aside from the broad strokes of the issue, many Americans likely don't fully understand how campaign finance law works or exactly what PACs and super PACs are. Let's therefore take a moment to lay out the salient factors at play here.

First, a PAC is a political action committee. Here is the definition according to the Federal Election Commission:

> The term 'political action committee' (PAC) refers to two distinct types of political committees registered with the FEC: separate segregated funds (SSFs) and nonconnected committees. Basically, SSFs are political committees established and administered by corporations, labor unions, membership organizations or trade associations. These committees can only solicit contributions from individuals associated with connected or sponsoring organization. By contrast, nonconnected committees – as their name suggests – are not sponsored by or connected to any of the aforementioned entities and are free to solicit contributions from the general public.[26]

These PACs are limited in certain types of spending. They can only give $5,000 to a candidate for a given election, with primaries and general elections counting as separate elections. They can also give up to $15,000 to a political party per year, and another $5,000 to a different PAC per year.

Previously, due to the 2002 Campaign Reform Act cosponsored by John McCain and Russ Feingold, these corporations and unions could not spend from their own funds on issues pertaining to campaigns. Now, because of the *Citizens United* decision, they not only can spend their money on independent ads and other activities, they can do so without limit, via what is called a super PAC. And what's more, they don't have to disclose how much they donate or to which cause. They can funnel unlimited amounts of dark money into influencing elections at every level of our democracy. The only hindrance on their powers in this regard is that they cannot coordinate directly with a candidate on these ads and other activities, though as many have observed, enforcing this is easier said than done.

Sanders is the only credible candidate running for president in regard to serious campaign finance reform, not just because he has the strongest stance on the issue but also because he doesn't have a super PAC and is running a campaign entirely funded by individual donors. He is not beholden to special interests because he hasn't accepted any of their money. Clinton cannot say the same, not by the tune of several million dollars.

Former president Jimmy Carter perhaps said it best when he said that this newly allowed, unlimited dark money

> violates the essence of what made America a great country in its political system. Now, it's just an oligarchy, with unlimited political bribery being the essence of getting the nominations for president or to elect the president. And the same thing applies to governors and U.S. Senators and congress members. So now we've just seen a complete subversion of our political system as a payoff to major contributors, who want and expect and sometimes get favors for themselves after the election's over.[27]

But are Carter and Sanders over-reacting? How much do these super PACs really spend? As it turns out, they spend absurdly large sums. It is estimated that the Koch brothers and their various organizations will spend $750 million in the 2016 election cycle. To put this in perspective, that is more than either the Democratic Party or Republican Party will spend, meaning that one family will have more influence, financially speaking, than either the major political parties.

If we really want a government of, by, and for the people of this country – if we really believe in the notion of *one person, one vote* – then we must enact tough campaign finance reform of the sort Sanders suggests, and he is the best candidate to get it done.

CRIMINAL JUSTICE REFORM

"Millions of lives have been destroyed because people are in jail for nonviolent crimes. For decades, we have been engaged in a failed "War on Drugs" with racially-biased mandatory minimums that punish people of color unfairly. It is an obscenity that we stigmatize so many young Americans with a criminal record for smoking marijuana, but not one major Wall Street executive has been prosecuted for causing the near collapse of our entire economy. This must change."
– Bernie Sanders[28]

It is a disgrace that the United States incarcerates more of its citizens than any other country on Earth. It is a further disgrace that those incarcerated are disproportionately minorities and poor. It is yet a further disgrace that while the millionaires and billionaires that destroyed our economy in 2008 are not only free but richer than ever before, young people's lives are being damaged, sometimes irreparably, by charges of marijuana possession. And finally the word *disgrace* is insufficient to the task of describing the ethical disaster that private for-profit prisons are. As Sanders phrases it:

> It is morally repugnant that we have privatized prisons all over America.

Corporations should not be allowed to make a profit by building more jails and keeping more Americans behind bars. We have got to end the private for-profit prison racket in America. Earlier this year, Sen. Sanders introduced legislation that will end the private prison industry.[29]

Bernie Sanders is the only presidential candidate on either side of the fence who takes criminal justice reform seriously, and he is the one who most frequently associates it with racial justice as well:

If current trends continue, one in four black males born today can expect to spend time in prison during their lifetime. Blacks are imprisoned at six times the rate of whites and a report by the Department of Justice found that blacks were three times more likely to be searched during a traffic stop, compared to white motorists. Together, African-Americans and Latinos comprised 57 percent of all prisoners in 2014, even though African-Americans and Latinos make up approximately one quarter of the U.S. population. These outcomes are not reflective of increased crime by communities of color, but rather a disparity in enforcement and reporting mechanisms. African-Americans are twice as likely to be arrested and almost four times as likely to experience the use of force during encounters with the police. [30]

Sanders sees also that while marijuana usage is roughly the same between blacks and whites, blacks are four times more likely to be arrested for possession. His solution here is a simple one: legalize marijuana, thus solving the racial problem in this one area, while also preventing young people of any race from ending up with a felony drug possession that could prevent employment later in life, financial aid for college, or even college admission in some cases. Once again, he is the only candidate to stand up for legalization, even though according to a 2015 Gallup poll 58 percent of Americans now support legalization.[31]

Sanders is also the only presidential candidate who seeks substantive reform in how we handle corporate criminals. Dealing with corporate crime is not only popular among the American people, it is essential if we are going to create a fair playing field instead of allowing our rigged economy to continue fixing the fight for the ultra-rich at the expense of the poor and middle-class.

But this is just one area where Sanders has the proper policies to correct our off-kilter economy. In the next chapter, we'll look at his broader economic plan more closely.

ECONOMIC POLICY

"No single financial institution should have holdings so extensive that its failure could send the world economy into another financial crisis [...] If an institution is too big to fail, it is too big to exist." – Bernie Sanders[32]

It is hard to imagine a stronger economic advocate for average Americans than Bernie Sanders. Elizabeth Warren might be the only other American public figure with an equal track record on the issue. He has led the way on regulating Wall Street, fighting tax breaks for the ultra-rich, supporting tax relief for working families, and protecting the impoverished from the excesses of the financial elite. In 2001 Sanders voted against the first round of Bush tax cuts, and in the 2003 he voted against the second round. These are tax cuts that will cost the U.S. government an estimated $3.2 trillion dollars between 2001 and 2021. Sanders supported Glass-Steagall, the repeal of which led to the deregulation of banking entities, thus allowing them to grow to outrageous size, becoming, as it is usually phrased, too big to fail. It was this deregulation that led to the 2008 economic collapse and the eventual need for the American people to bail out Wall Street at enormous expense. He voted for Dodd-Frank, but had this to say about it: "Let's not kid ourselves. Dodd-Frank was a very modest piece of legislation. Dodd-Frank did not end much of the casino-style gambling on Wall Street." [33]

Seeing that Dodd-Frank was not sufficient to reign in Wall Street's excesses, Sanders currently supports a revised version of Glass-Steagall, a position recently endorsed by 170 top economists. [34]

While some of the positions Sanders holds – such as his leadership on reigning in Wall Street – have become topics for big media outlets and liberal activists, it should be noted that he tackles lesser-known problems and proposes bold and innovative new programs to solve day-to-day problems for Americans of all walks of life and from every region in the country.

For example, in 2009 Sanders successfully added an amendment to an agricultural appropriations bill that increased funding for the Farm Service Agency by $350 million dollars, specifically to aid small dairy farmers struggling to compete against massive agribusiness. This support for small business in rural areas might not make headline news, but it affects hundreds of thousands of Americans all over the country.

Sanders is likewise strong on many other forms of small business. He also has innovative new ideas, like his recent proposal to allow post offices to act as banks, thus helping the most impoverished who can't obtain a banking account and are therefore forced to cash their checks at a loss to predatory financial entities. This proposal would benefit many inner-city workers in largely African-American communities. Sanders's past successes and proposals for future legislation help a wide array of Americans who most need it, from rural Vermonters to inner-city Chicagoans and a dozen stations in between.

The final point that should be covered is that many on the right have argued that Sanders could not pay for his various social programs, such as expanding Social Security, making state college tuition free, investing in our infrastructure, and offering universal healthcare. Indeed, it does sound like a tall order, but he has proposed two key measures to pay for all of his programs that would help a vast majority of Americans.

First, he has proposed raising the minimum income ceiling on Social Security to $250,000 from its current $118,500:

> Doing so would impact only the top 1.5
> percent of wage earners, the Center for

Economic Policy Research has estimated [....] Asking the wealthiest Americans to contribute more into Social Security, would not only extend the solvency of Social Security through 2060, it also would allow Social Security benefits to be expanded for millions of Americans.[35]

This plan is unimpeachable, since Social Security works from a different money stream than do regular budgetary concerns. Sanders's proposal would therefore pay for itself without a problem.

The other major proposal for raising funds for his programs is to instate a transaction tax on all Wall Street speculation. Here is the proposal in Sanders's own words:

My legislation would impose a Wall Street speculation fee of 0.5 percent on stock trades (that's 50 cents for every $100 worth of stock), a 0.1 percent fee on bonds, and a 0.005 percent fee on derivatives. It has been estimated that this legislation would raise up to $300 billion a year. [36]

If this sort of tax on Wall Street sounds far-fetched to you, it shouldn't. Over one thousand American economists have endorsed the plan, and it is popular among the American people as well.

What's more, over forty countries worldwide –
including such economic powerhouses as Britain,
Germany, France, Switzerland, and China – have
adopted a similar tax on speculation. We therefore
have demonstrable proof that this policy works
in dozens of countries all over the world, ranging
from small and impoverished countries to large
and rich countries; Western countries and Eastern
countries; countries in the Northern Hemisphere
and the Southern Hemisphere. In short, the support
for this policy is overwhelming, as is the proof of its
efficacy.

But how much money would it actually bring
in? An estimated $350 billion per year, money that
would go a long way toward paying for the social
programs Sanders is proposing.

I would also like to reiterate what I said
about raising the minimum wage in the chapter on
democratic socialism. Raising the minimum wage
not only helps those workers who see an increase
in their financial standing, but it also it improves
the economy as a whole because money trickles
up, not down. All of the cities and states that have
raised the minimum wage have seen corollary job
growth afterward. This increase in buying power
improves lives immediately and creates new jobs,
but it also leads to an increase in tax revenue which

would further help Sanders pay for his proposed social programs. It should also be mentioned that in January 2016, 70 percent of new jobs added in the United States were minimum wage restaurant or retail jobs, meaning that more and more of the American workforce is living off minimum wage.[37] If our economy is shifting more toward minimum wage positions, as many indications show, it is more urgent than ever to make the minimum a living wage.

In conclusion, the reason we should support Sanders's economic policies is three-fold. First, Sanders has proven that he thinks boldly and accurately about all sectors of the economy – from Wall Street to Main Street, from urban areas to rural areas, here at home and abroad. Second, he has proven willing and capable of standing up to big interests in favor of protecting the middle class and the impoverished. Third, his policies are the only ones that will reverse our ruinous trajectory whereby wealth and income inequality grows unchecked and has been doing so for decades. He is therefore the best candidate in every respect vis-à-vis the economy.

EDUCATION POLICY

"If you think education is expensive – try ignorance."
– Ann Landers[38]

We are in the midst of a crisis in higher education the likes of which our country has never before faced. Tuition is at an all-time high; student loan debt has reached astronomical proportions; over 70 percent of classes are taught by overworked and underpaid adjunct instructors (for those who don't know what an adjunct is, it is an instructor hired semester-by-semester with little or no job security, sadly low wages, no power within the academic institution, and often no benefits of any kind); and job prospects for many alumni of four-year and graduate programs range from difficult to dismal. Not only must our current trajectory be halted, it must be radically reversed.

Bernie Sanders has long been a leader on controlling costs for higher education and reducing student loan debt, and unlike other candidates appear to, he takes the issue seriously:

> Over the next decade, it has been estimated that the federal government will make a profit of over $110 billion on

student loan programs. This is morally wrong and it is bad economics. As President, Sen. Sanders will prevent the federal government from profiteering on the backs of college students and use this money instead to significantly lower student loan interest rates. [39]

He has also opposed predatory for-profit universities, a growing epidemic few in this country are aware of. As Elizabeth Warren writes:

[Education Management Corporation] signed up tens of thousands of students by lying about its programs, it saddled them with fraudulent degrees and huge debts. Those debts wrecked lives. Under the law, the government can bar such institutions from receiving more federal student loans. But EDMC just paid a fine and kept right on raking in federal loan money. [40]

And the EDMC is just one of many such predatory institutions at work today. Sanders's strong opposition to these entities and their unethical practices is an important step toward restoring our higher education system. Getting profit out of education altogether is another.

As I mentioned in the previous chapter, Sanders has proposed a sensible means of paying for free college tuition, but what would it look like to have free higher education? I will be honest here, as I promised to be in the preface of this book: no one knows exactly, and the change would likely not happen overnight. One thing that is certain is that potential students who are capable of attending college would be able to, thus helping to reverse our slide down the international rankings in terms of advanced literacy, math, and science. All of the countries currently beating the U.S. in these rankings have tuition-free (or close to tuition-free) higher education, and this is no coincidence. When a nation invests in its education, its education improves, and when colleges are not high-dollar diploma mills, but rather actual institutions of learning, it turns out that students receive a better education.

Another clear outcome of increased attendance at colleges and universities would be more work for the increasing number of Americans with graduate degrees who want to pay their education forward via teaching. There is no guarantee that this increase would be in terms of tenure-track or full-time professorships, of course, but the larger demand for instructors would at minimum create guarantees of employment, even if at the adjunct level. My hope is that we would see more stable positions open up, but here again I have to be honest and say that this might be a different fight once we've crossed that bridge.

Sanders knows his proposals will require a fight, but at least he is fighting to moving us in the right direction. Reducing student loan debt, reducing predatory practices among for-profit universities, and moving us toward a tuition-free higher education are necessary if we want to remain competitive on the global market. They are also the ethical things to do.

But it's not just our higher education system that is in turmoil these days, and Sanders doesn't ignore early-childhood education or secondary school education. He has been a particularly strong opponent of George W. Bush's No Child Left Behind law. As he answered in the candidate's questionnaire from the AFT teachers' union:

> I voted against No Child Left Behind in 2001, and continue to oppose the bill's reliance on high-stakes standardized testing to direct draconian interventions. In my view, No Child Left Behind ignores several important factors in a student's academic performance, specifically the

impact of poverty, access to adequate health care, mental health, nutrition, and a wide variety of supports that children in poverty should have access to. By placing so much emphasis on standardized testing, No Child Left Behind ignores many of the skills and qualities that are vitally important in our 21st century economy, like problem solving, critical thinking, and teamwork, in favor of test preparation that provides no benefit to students after they leave school.[41]

And the overwhelming majority of teachers are in support of Sanders's position. A recent poll of educators found that just one percent of them thought that NCLB evaluation techniques were "an effective way to assess the quality of schools."[42] Americans overall also give the law a bad grade, regardless of political affiliation. Among Republicans, only 18 percent said it makes education better, while 29 percent said it makes education worse, with 38 percent saying it's not made much difference. Among Independents, 14 percent said it makes education better, while 32 percent said it makes education worse, with 35 percent saying it's not made much difference.

Among Democrats, 17 percent said it makes education better, while 26 percent said it makes education worse, with 43 percent saying it's not made much difference.[43]

In effect, those most familiar with the law – that is, the teachers who are affected by it daily – find it abysmal, and average Americans across the political spectrum likewise find it notably more negative than positive.

Sanders is not just paying lip-service here. He has helped rewrite the law and has been active in the broader fight on education. He is knowledgeable in a nuanced way and concerned about the issue from several angles:

> I believe the Alexander-Murray compromise on No Child Left Behind reauthorization represents a step in the right direction, and voted for the bill in Committee. While this legislation could go much further to provide adequate resources to our lowest-income students, I believe it is an important step forward. I strongly oppose the Student Success Act because it would gut the core provisions of federal law that direct education funding toward the low-income students who need it most.[44]

This is not a senator who has his staff read bills without his having looked at them. This is a senator who takes a hands-on approach and knows the issues before him.

As we read more about Sanders's positions on primary and secondary education, we learn that he has lofty philosophical notions, highly practical proposals for improving teacher training and student success, and an ethical compass that doesn't fail him. The same is true of his positions on higher education. We need to revitalize our education system from top to bottom if we want to have a truly educated populace that can compete in the global market, understand the social and political issues facing us today, and enjoy all the emotional and intellectual enrichment education brings with it. Sanders has the correct plans to bring this about. We should therefore adopt his positions and support his candidacy in this election cycle, but we must also fight to make his positions the accepted ones across the country, which is something he will need if he is elected, and something our country needs no matter who is elected.

ENVIRONMENTAL POLICY

"This is not a question of one nation or two nations. This is a question of humanity." – Dalai Lama[45]

Despite the environment being one of the major concerns facing voters today, we can keep this section incredibly brief, given the level of clarity regarding Sanders's positions and record on the environment and climate change. Bernie Sanders has an impeccable record on the environment, receiving high marks from environmentalist groups and leading the charge on many key issues. Sanders has been against the Keystone pipeline from day one, has proposed legislation that would impose a carbon tax on corporate polluters, and is the only presidential candidate who opposes fracking. Sanders enjoys a 95 percent lifetime rating from the League of Conservation voters.[46] And as Ben Adler writes:

> Sanders has one of the strongest climate change records in the Senate. In fact, according to rankings released by Climate Hawks Vote, a new super PAC, Sanders was the No. 1 climate leader in the Senate for the 113th Congress.[47]

His voting record and proposals on the issue of the environment are as good as it gets. As I promised in the preface to this book, however, I will hold myself to a high standard of intellectual honesty. I will therefore say that this is one area where Clinton has a strong record as well – not as strong as that of Sanders, but still rather strong. The main concerns are her ties to Big Oil, her lack of opposition to fracking, and her muddled position on the Keystone pipeline.

Sanders has also gone further in his claims about the importance of climate change, calling it the greatest threat facing the planet today. Here again, Sanders is the candidate for this moment in history. The global community is waking up to the real threat of climate change, as evidenced by the United Nations COP21 summit from November 30 to December 11 of 2015. A historic number of nations took part in the summit and a general consensus on the threat of climate change was reached:

> For the first time ever, 195 nations fully agreed on the science of climate change [...] for the first time, nations acknowledged collective responsibility for addressing the problem. [48]

If the United States wants to be a leader on climate change – and a leader in new technologies that will bring in billions of dollars over the coming decades – we need a president who understands the magnitude of the issue and is willing to put it front and center in our nation's political discourse. Bernie Sanders would clearly be that president. It is questionable whether Hillary Clinton would be.

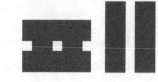

FOREIGN POLICY

"I was opposed to Iraq from the start, and I say that not just to look backwards, but also to look forwards, because I think what the next president has to show is the kind of judgment that will ensure that we are using our military power wisely."
– Barack Obama[49]

One of the regular claims Clinton supporters make is that she is more experienced than Sanders when it comes to foreign policy due to her years as secretary of state. First off, I would argue that Sanders's years in the Senate have given him sufficient foreign policy experience to be president of the United States, but perhaps more important than the quantity of each candidate's experience is the quality of their judgment on foreign policy matters. Let's look at the single most important foreign policy decision anyone has had to make in the twenty-first century: the Iraq War.

Clinton has reversed herself and apologized for her vote for the Iraq War, and her supporters want us think this is enough to set the matter aside. A more thorough analysis of the situation, however, reveals major problems for Clinton. There are three options for explaining her vote, and none of them are good.

1) Clinton looked at the polling numbers and made a cynical vote to be in step with the polling she saw.

2) Clinton was eyeing the presidency and believed, as many Democrats did at the time, that a vote against the Iraq War would damage her chances of winning the presidency, and so she made a cynical vote to ensure her political future.

3) Clinton honestly supported the war and thought it was a good idea.

Of these three options, the first two are damning since they might mean that Clinton cared more for her own political standing than the lives of Americans, our allies, and Iraqis. The third option might be the most damning, however, since it suggests Clinton has a problem of vision. It would mean she saw all the same information about the region that Sanders did and didn't realize a war in Iraq would destabilize the region and lead to a costly quagmire.

Now let's look at Sanders on the issue. Here is his speech from Senate floor:

> Mr. Speaker, I do not think any Member
> of this body disagrees that Saddam
> Hussein is a tyrant, a murderer, and
> a man who has started two wars. He
> is clearly someone who cannot be
> trusted or believed. The question, Mr.
> Speaker, is not whether we like Saddam
> Hussein or not. The question is whether
> he represents an imminent threat to
> the American people and whether a
> unilateral invasion of Iraq will do more
> harm than good.

All of that is reasonable stuff and I'm glad Sanders said it, but here's where he becomes uncannily prescient about the matter.

> I am concerned about the problems of
> so-called unintended consequences.
> Who will govern Iraq when Saddam
> Hussein is removed and what role will
> the U.S. play in ensuing a civil war that
> could develop in that country? Will
> moderate governments in the region
> who have large Islamic fundamentalist
> populations be overthrown and replaced
> by extremists? [50]

Sanders also spoke to the outrageous financial cost of the war and the danger to U.S. troops. He was therefore entirely correct in his assessment. He saw the ethical, financial, and geopolitical consequences of the Iraq War in a way that Clinton either did not see or did not care about because she had more pressing career concerns. And I reiterate that it doesn't matter which explanation you prefer for Clinton's ill-advised vote; any among them is equally damning.

But we shouldn't merely re-adjudicate the past. We have to ask what kind of foreign policy Sanders would have for the future. Here he is discussing his Middle East strategy:

> I find it remarkable that Saudi Arabia, which borders Iraq and is controlled by a multi-billion dollar family, is demanding that U.S. combat troops have "boots on the ground" against ISIS. Where are the Saudi troops? With the third largest military budget in the world and an army far larger than ISIS, the Saudi government must accept its full responsibility for stability in their own region of the world. Ultimately, this is a profound struggle for the soul of Islam, and the anti-ISIS Muslim nations must lead that fight. While the United States and other western nations should be

supportive, the Muslim nations must lead. [51]

Sanders has repeatedly called for the oil-rich countries of the Middle East that claim to be our allies to step up and put real resources into reducing terrorism and conflict in their own region, with Western allies as support when necessary. This action would deflate the image of the United States as an imperialist power, an image that terrorist groups use to great effect when recruiting new members.

In effect, not only has Sanders shown remarkable judgment in the past, a Sanders presidency could finally put an end to neoliberal and neoconservative policies alike, whereas a Clinton presidency would extend and perhaps even expand them.

GUN CONTROL

"I think there is consensus for serious gun control, including among people who own guns. And I think that's what we have to bring about." – Bernie Sanders[52]

We have all heard various disturbing statistics about gun violence in the United States, but they bear repeating and holding long in the mind. Let's merely look at 2015 as a snapshot of where we are as a nation in regard to gun violence.

> There were 372 mass shootings in the U.S. in 2015, killing 475 people and wounding 1,870 [...] A mass shooting is defined as a single shooting incident which kills or injures four or more people, including the assailant.[53]

This means we had more than one mass shooting per day, which rightly shocks and horrifies many, but what is even more shocking is that these mass shootings that attract so much media attention only account for 3.5 percent of the shooting deaths that occurred in 2015, since "some 13,286 people were killed in the U.S. by firearms in 2015 [...] and 26,819 people were injured."[54] I ask you to pause and let this information take full and permanent root in your imagination: despite having more than one mass shooting per day in 2015, those deaths represent only 3.5 percent of shooting deaths, and shooting deaths occurred at an average rate of 1.5 per hour every day of the year.

Once you've processed that, you have to then realize that while homicides get the vast majority of attention in the media and our culture as a whole, 60 percent of total gun deaths are suicides. This means that gun deaths are not only a public safety and law enforcement issue, but also a mental health issue. It also means that when people talk of criminals getting guns, they miss the point that criminals or madmen with machine guns actually comprise a tiny fraction of gun-related deaths in the United States.

Our country experiences greater and more frequent loss of life due to firearms than any other country on Earth by a wide margin. The next president will have to tackle this issue head-on and bring our nation forward to a sane and functional gun control policy. The question is: who is the best candidate to achieve this absolutely necessary goal? Clinton and her surrogates have repeatedly tried to paint Sanders as the NRA candidate. Thus far it doesn't seem to have taken hold and hasn't damaged Sanders in any significant way. I want to explain why this line of attack from Clinton has largely failed and why Sanders is in fact the better candidate to enact progressive gun control legislation.

The main reason Clinton's attacks have failed is that they are generally inaccurate. Sanders has a D- rating from the NRA, so painting him as the NRA's candidate immediately rings false to voters. But even among those voters who would prefer to see Sanders be more aggressive on gun control, I think the attacks fail for a different reason. Most Americans agree with Sanders that "99.9 percent of [gun owners] obey the law."[55] We also tend to see a massive difference between rural areas and urban areas in regard to gun ownership and use, because in rural areas guns tend to be for sporting purposes such as hunting or target shooting, whereas in urban areas their sole use is to harm other human beings. Sanders comes from a rural state, and despite Clinton's attempts to ignore this fact, Americans have not.

But there is another reason Sanders's somewhat more moderate position on gun control has not hurt him among voters. Even those of us who might want to see harsher laws on the issue than perhaps Sanders himself would support realize that he is uniquely positioned to make progress on this issue. As a senator from a rural state, he can talk to that demographic of gun owners in their language and on their terms, thus bringing together a coalition that can get all of the reasonable controls Sanders has proposed passed. And what are his specific proposals on gun control?

Since 1988, when he first ran for a U.S. congressional seat, Sanders has supported a ban on assault weapons. He also supports instant background checks to prevent felons from purchasing firearms. He supports closing the gun-show loophole to background checks. He also supports mental health checks for purchasing guns, which could prevent many of the aforementioned suicides and likely quite a few of the aforementioned mass shootings.[56] These are all measures a majority of Americans agree with by large margins, with 80 percent of Americans wanting tougher gun laws in general.[57]

Despite all of these entirely reasonable and achievable policy positions, some voters might still have doubts or might believe the attacks from the Clinton camp. We should therefore think more carefully about the votes Sanders has cast that trouble some people. It serves no one to hide the facts. The most frequently cited issue with

Sanders's record is that he has voted several times to protect gun sellers from liability in the case of accidental or purposeful shootings. Most liberals are intensely in support of holding these entities accountable in such cases, but Sanders has a philosophically rigorous reason for having opposed this approach. He argues that if a small business sells you a gun legally, and you then go out and shoot someone with it, the fault lies with you, not the gun shop owners.

Interestingly, this same legal thinking applies to literally every other product sold in the United States – cars, knives, baseball bats, et cetera. Why should we single out this one product?, Sanders seems to be asking. His position is therefore philosophically consistent with commerce practices across the board. I would also add that if his gun control policies were to be enacted, what can be legally sold and to whom would change much for the better, thus reducing the problems that have led to many calling for legislation that holds gun sellers liable.

The answer to the earlier question of who is the best candidate to make progress on gun control is therefore Sanders, because he will be able to bring together a diverse coalition to enact what a vast majority of Americans want in regard to gun control. He also has decades of experience dealing the issue as both a mayor who worked with law enforcement and later as a congress member representing a rural state. His position is therefore philosophically consistent and politically viable.

INFRASTRUCTURE

"The American Society of Civil Engineers said in 2007 that the U.S. had fallen so far behind in maintaining its public infrastructure—roads, bridges, schools, dams—that it would take more than a trillion and half dollars over five years to bring it back up to standard. Instead, these types of expenditures are being cut back. At the same time, public infrastructure around the world is facing unprecedented stress, with hurricanes, cyclones, floods and forest fires all increasing in frequency and intensity." – Naomi Klein[58]

In 2013 the American Society of Civil Engineers raised America's infrastructure grade to a D+. Yes, you read that correctly: *raised* it to a D+. When we look at the facts, we shouldn't be surprised to hear that our rating is so low. Of the roughly 600,000 bridges in the country, nearly 25 percent of them "have been designated as structurally deficient or functionally obsolete."[59] And it's not just our bridges. Our sewage systems and networks of water pipes are sometimes decades into disrepair, leading to inefficient transmission of potable water and accidental pollution. Our public transit is the worst in the industrialized world, trailing badly behind all Western European countries and also behind China, Japan, Korea, and much of Russia.

Sanders has therefore proposed spending $1.3 trillion dollars on infrastructure, which he argues will create 13 million jobs, help safeguard the environment, and save lives. I want to focus specifically on public transit, since it receives the least air-time in political debates.

The first thing to consider when looking at the economics of public transit is that it creates jobs that cannot be outsourced. The ticket inspector, the train conductor or bus driver, the repair crews for railways, the mechanics who perform regular repairs and safety checks, and the staff at train stations and bus depots are all employees that must be physically located in the United States and, more specifically, in their home regions and cities. But it is not just that these are stable jobs with government benefits that will improve the lives of these workers directly. A recent study shows that investing in local public transit has a noticeably positive effect on the local economy overall; according to the American Public Transportation Association, every tax dollar invested in passenger trains yields nearly four dollars in local economic growth.[60]

But the economic gains don't stop there. In terms of alleviating the disadvantages that come with income inequality, public transit can be helpful as well. For example, Champaign-Urbana, Illinois, offers a year-long pass with unlimited rides on the city buses for only $70, an amount a worker might pay in a single week if dependent on taxis or services like Uber. Another example: Chapel Hill, North Carolina, offers bus service for free, thus eliminating any financial burden for poor workers needing to get to work. This means that workers who can't afford a car or can't drive a car due to a disability or illness can still hold a job and earn an income.

And it's not just the poor who can benefit here. According to The Transit Savings Report, a monthly analysis produced by the American Public Transportation Association, public transit can save users an average of $764 per month, or about $9,167 a year.[61] With the middle class getting hit right, left, and center with increasing college tuition, decreasing or stagnating wages, and ever-increasing economic precariousness, these savings are not merely nominal but necessary.

Congestion alone costs us billions of dollars per year. According to a recent U.S. News & World Report article: "The cost of congestion to the average auto commuter was $960 in lost time and fuel in 2014, compared to an inflation-adjusted

$400 in 1982." And overall costs nationwide are expected to balloon: "In the next five years, the annual delay per commuter would grow from 42 to 47 hours, the total delay nationwide would grow from 6.9 billion hours to 8.3 billion hours, and the total cost of congestion would jump from $160 billion to $192 billion, researchers estimated." [62]

Funding public transit is therefore a great economic boon for the United States in terms of saving money for commuters, helping the poor, and creating general economic growth. But we have to think about more than economics when determining public policy. In many ways, the most pressing matter facing us as a species is the environment, since if we don't reverse our policies that are destroying the planet we rely on for nourishment and breathable air, we won't have the opportunity to solve any of the other problems that face us. Here again, public transit can help. Trains are 17 percent more efficient as a means of travel than airplanes and 34 percent more efficient than cars – and that's in the current state American trains are in. If we were to modernize all of our passenger trains and invest in new technologies to improve fuel efficiency, while also increasing the number of people who rely on trains as their primary mode of commuter and long-distance travel, the positive impact on our environment could be colossal.

It should also be mentioned that both liberals and conservatives in this country regularly use the catch-phrase "energy independence." I by no means believe that public transit, including electric trains and biodiesel buses, can allow us to achieve complete energy independence, but by reducing our need for petroleum energy sources, we can make great strides not only in protecting our environment but also in reducing our need to purchase oil from countries in the Middle East. And since liberals, moderates, and conservatives alike agree that energy independence is desirable, this could be a major selling point for increased public transit and for Sanders as a candidate.

The facts are overwhelming, but can we convince Americans to embrace public transit in significant ways? According to the data on Amtrak usage, we already are convincing them. The popularity of Amtrak has increased notably since the 2008 economic crisis. Take Alabama as an example. In 2008, the National Association of Railroad Passengers reported 47,399 passengers in the state. In 2010 that number had grown to 62,737, and in 2014 the number was 62,426. This represents a 32 percent increase in passengers that has remained steady, and this number is even more striking given that Alabama is generally ranked rather poorly in terms of its public transportation. And we saw similar increases across the nation. In Ohio the increase from 2008 to 2014 was 119,000 to 152,000. In Illinois the number increased from 4,295,300 to 4,883,900 – meaning that over half a million more passengers rode Amtrak in 2014 than in 2008. In Pennsylvania a quarter million more passengers used Amtrak in 2014 than in 2008. I won't enumerate each state's increases, but suffice it to say that these increases have occurred across the United States and have remained steady over the past half-decade. It is therefore irrefutable that we are seeing greater demand for public transportation in this country; all that remains is to muster the political willpower to make it more widely available and more affordable.

By investing in public transit, bridge and highway repair, waterworks updates, and similar projects, Sanders will improve the state of the nation's infrastructure and create hundreds of millions of jobs, representing the largest improvements of this kind since FDR's administration. And even though infrastructure is not a particularly sexy topic, it is one of the most important facing us, since it links into the economy, the environment, and quality of life in so many ways. Sanders is the only presidential candidate offering a comprehensive plan to invest in our infrastructure, and though it is unlikely to be the main selling point for his candidacy, it should sway thinking voters into his camp.

BERNIE SANDERS AND IDENTITY POLITICS

"I don't vote with my vagina [...] It's so insulting to women to think that [we] would follow a candidate just because she's a woman." – Susan Sarandon[63]

For some time now, perhaps the most dominant concern among liberal circles has been identity politics, likely dating back to the 1990s. This concern has only increased in dominance over the past decade, especially in the recent years. With a powerful new wave of feminism sweeping over the country, LGBTQ battles being fought and won in the courts, and the #BlackLivesMatter movement gaining ever more visibility and political viability, we truly are in an age of identity politics unlike ever before. And the role social media has played in this sea-swell of unrest and protest cannot be underestimated.

So, how does a white septuagenarian male fit into this age? Hillary Clinton, her surrogates, and too many of her supporters have all implicitly or explicitly stated that supporting Bernie Sanders is sexist or that the only way to be truly feminist is to vote for Clinton. I won't embark on an exhaustive

(and exhausting) laundry list of women and
minorities who support Sanders, but I do want to
take this criticism seriously and offer a serious
defense of Sanders and his movement along the
lines of identity politics.

Since Clinton and her supporters have
attacked the Sanders movement along the lines of
sex, I'll address this issue first. Sanders has long
identified as a feminist and has an impeccable track
record on women's rights – so much so in fact, that
Gloria Steinem declared him an "honorary woman"
in 1996. [64] It is also worth noting that Sanders
has received many more donations from women
than Clinton has. [65] And, finally, there has been a
parade of prominent feminists and female actors,
politicians, and public figures to have thrown
their support behind Sanders. Actress and liberal
activist Susan Sarandon has urged female voters
not to support Clinton simply because she is a
woman, but rather to vote for Sanders because his
policies are superior and he is not beholden to big-
money interests. [66] Sanders also has a 100 percent
rating from NARAL.[67]

In short, as all the facts suggest, it is
inaccurate to say Sanders has weak support among
women or that his candidacy represents anything
but a strong feminist agenda. Some among us

might wish that Elizabeth Warren had run, so that we could have both Sanders's policies and elect a woman to the White House – which it's about damn time we did – but for right now, Sanders is not only our best candidate in terms of policy but also in terms of diversity.

Why would I say that he is our best candidate in terms of diversity? There are several reasons. First and foremost, we have to look at his record on the issues. Sanders supported gay rights long before it was popular even among Democrats:

> By all measures, Sanders was ahead of his time in supporting gay rights. In 1983, as mayor of Burlington, he signed a Gay Pride Day proclamation calling it a civil rights issue. He was one of just 67 members in the House of Representatives to vote against the Defense of Marriage Act, a politically tough decision he prides himself on and points to as a key progressive bona fide. Sanders opposed Don't Ask Don't Tell in 1993, another President Bill Clinton-era policy, and supported civil unions in Vermont in 2000. [68]

I also invite everyone to search "Bernie Sanders defends gay soldiers, 1995" on YouTube to hear his spirited defense of gays in the military. Just listen to the authentic outrage in his voice as he defends these brave men and women against bigoted attacks. Listen to him and you will feel the depth of his convictions on this issue two decades before the Supreme Court made same-sex marriage legal. (Side note: I describe the men and women as *brave* not because of the usual jingoism that insists we describe all soldiers in such terms, but rather because being gay in the military requires a special kind of courage.)

As queer studies scholar Dr. Chase Dimock writes of Sanders's long-standing support for LGBTQ rights:

> The above image is of Bernie's declaration of a "Gay Pride Day" in Burlington, VT in 1985. I was born in 1985, which means that this man has been advocating for my civil rights my entire life. As we near the democratic primaries, I believe it is important for the LGBT community to consider the value of such a long history of support. I don't want to vote for a candidate that only chose to recognize my humanity when it became politically expedient. I want to vote for a candidate who has been standing up for me since day one. [69]

There is no better way to say it than Dr. Dimock has. Sanders has been a staunch supporter of LGBTQ rights longer than any major politician in this country. This mirrors his long-term commitment to black rights and solidifies his record on civil rights issues in ways that Clinton can't hope to compete with.

It would be impossible to discuss diversity and racial justice at this juncture in history without mentioning the #BlackLivesMatter movement. The clearest distinction between Sanders and Clinton in terms of the #BlackLivesMatter movement is that after Ferguson, Sanders hired Symone Sanders (no relation to Bernie Sanders) as his national press secretary. Symone Sanders was a major part of the #BlackLivesMatter movement, and her hire was a clear show of support for the importance of that movement to Bernie Sanders. Clinton, on the other hand, went to a black church in Ferguson and declared that "all lives matter." This difference in response to the unjustified shootings of black people around the United States encapsulates the real difference between the candidates. Sanders takes bold action to change things in this country, while Clinton at best pays lip-service, and often rather gauche lip-service, to our problems.

I don't mean to suggest that this one factor should entirely determine voters' reactions to the two candidates. Everyone should look into Sanders's voting record on matters that affect minority populations; I am confident that when you do, you will find that he has been there from day one, fighting for equality at every level for every American. I feel certain that when more people look into his stances and get to know Sanders better they will realize that he is the superior candidate on these issues. The media has discussed Sanders's supposed race problem, especially in regard to winning in South Carolina and Nevada, but I argue that this is an illusion. Sanders doesn't have a race problem, he has a name-recognition problem. As voters in these states and around the country get to know him, they sway his direction. This is how he has reduced Clinton's national lead from 31 percent to 2 percent in just a few short weeks from mid-December to early February.[70] And we are seeing similar shifts among all demographics.

It is also worth noting that many of the policy changes Sanders has proposed would help minorities and women in perhaps unexpected ways. Blacks, Latinos, and women are more likely to earn minimum wage than white men. Sanders's proposal to increase the minimum wage to $15 an hour over several years would therefore benefit these marginalized groups more greatly. [71] These same groups are also less likely to have strong retirement savings. This fact means that his proposal to strengthen Social Security would also benefit these groups more greatly. And, as I mentioned in the chapter on infrastructure, support for public transit helps the poor and minorities in ways the average American might not initially realize.

Clearly there are issues beyond economics that affect oppressed people – racial profiling, sexism and assault in women's daily lives, and the list goes on – but it would be wrong-minded to think that these economic changes wouldn't ameliorate their situation. Combating racism and sexism in the United States is a complicated matter, which Sanders understands, but reversing economic inequality is one of the primary ways to win the battle.

And Sanders's stances on diversity include the personal as much as the political (if in fact those two categories are separate at all). Earlier in this book, I mentioned Sanders's family life. I would like to return to this topic briefly. His parents were born in different countries – his father in Poland and his mother in the United States. His wife, her children, and her children's children are from a Catholic background, whereas Sanders himself is from a Jewish background. His son, Levi Sanders, has three adopted children from China. Are you beginning to see the picture I am painting here? The Sanders family is one that includes various nationalities, races, and religions. Diversity is part and parcel of his heritage and daily life. I don't want to make too much of this familial diversity, and I don't want to overplay the contrast with Clinton's mono-religious and mono-racial family, but I think it is worth noting. His policies are what we should focus on, and they clearly tell a story of a man dedicated to diversity. I merely want to suggest that his family life tells the same story as his political life, but from a more personal angle.

I hope I have made it clear that supporting Sanders is a show of support for a politics of equality and justice for all – regardless of gender, race, or religion. I do, however, hope that if he wins the Democratic nomination, Sanders will pick a woman or person of color as his running mate. I am with others who would love to see Elizabeth Warren run with him, but Tammy Baldwin of Wisconsin would also be a great choice, as would several others.

Here again, as I mentioned earlier in this book, since Sanders tends to listen to his supporters, it is incumbent upon us to make our voices heard on this matter – though, given his remarkable track record on issues of diversity, I doubt Sanders will need much convincing that his cabinet should be one of the most diverse in U.S. history, and I trust him to make the best decisions possible about all of his cabinet members based on their qualifications and the broader social concerns of identity politics.

THE PATH TO VICTORY

"Delegates are not the noblest sons and daughters of the Republic; a person of taste, arrived from Mars, would take one look at the convention floor and leave forever, convinced he had seen one of the drearier squats of hell. If one still smells the faint living echo of a carnival, it is regurgitated by the senses into the fouler cud of a death gas one must rid oneself of [...] The delegate is prepared for this office of selection by emptying wastebaskets, toting garbage, and saying yes at the right time for twenty years in the small political machine of some small or large town." – Norman Mailer[72]

The primary difference (pun intended) between the way the Democratic and Republican nomination processes work is that when a Republican wins a state, she or he takes 100 percent of the delegates from that state in the majority of cases (only states holding primaries between March 1 and March 14 this election cycle will dole out delegates proportionally), whereas Democrats always split the delegates proportionally by percentage of votes won. This is a situation that overall benefits Sanders but also presents some challenges. It also should determine our strategy for getting him elected and our strategy in case he doesn't win the nomination. Let me explain; but first, let me talk about superdelegates.

Clinton currently has 359 superdelegates, while Sanders currently has 29. What does that mean? What are superdelegates? The bluntest answer I can give is that they are one more part of the Electoral College that is demonstrably anti-democratic:

> Superdelegates are important because they can back any candidate they want, regardless of what the voters decide. So if Mr. Sanders, Ms. Clinton's top challenger, were to defy the odds and do damage to Ms. Clinton in New York, the superdelegates could at least blunt some of his success.[73]

And who are the lucky people who get to hold these positions? Let's take Clinton's state of New York as our example again:

> Superdelegates include former President Bill Clinton, Gov. Andrew Cuomo, both U.S. senators, all Democrat members of the House from New York, and members of the DNC, including Clinton backers like Jennifer Cunningham, Jay Jacobs and Maria Cuomo Cole.[74]

So, a former president, who happens to be Clinton's husband, and other high-ranking establishment figures in the Democratic Party. And no matter how the voters vote, these superdelegates can simply ignore the vote and weigh in on Clinton's behalf.

So, why do I bring up superdelegates right after explaining the way regular delegates are doled out based on percentages of votes? Because Clinton's establishment superdelegate advantage means we have to win considerably more regular delegates the old-fashioned way: by getting more votes from the people. So, with this perhaps new information about superdelegates in mind, let's return the way the Democratic primary process of proportionally doling out delegates should influence our strategy throughout the campaign season.

The way I see it, there are four ways Sanders can win the primary season, in the sense that there are three outcomes that I would consider a win for the Sanders movement:

> 1) He can simply outright win the nomination. This is of course my preferred outcome.

> 2) He can control the national discourse so much that Clinton has to adopt many

of his policy positions. We have already seen this happen time and again, so in a sense we've already won in this regard. The problem with this outcome, however, is that just as easily as she switched to his positions, she can switch back to her right-of-center tendencies.

3) He can accrue so many delegates that even if he doesn't win the nomination, the Democratic National Convention will be so packed with Sanders Democrats that the official DNC platform for 2016 will be as much a Sanders platform as a Clinton platform.

Since by my estimation we have already won with regard to outcome two, I want us to focus on outcomes one and three and how we need to make them happen.

Given the superdelegate situation, Sanders is going to have to outperform Clinton in voting. Here we all have to fight for the Sanders campaign in the most effective ways. I argue that the Sanders campaign model of relying on small donations and hundreds of thousands of volunteers is the best possible model, if we can in fact keep it going and growing. This happens in only one way: we have to commit to donating regularly, even if in small amounts, and we have to commit to volunteering several hours a month – nothing herculean, but definitely consistent – in order to make sure the movement and its momentum reach such an unbeatable level. For example, we could commit to not eating out more than once or twice a week to save about $50 a week, half of which we could donate to Sanders and half of which we could put in savings. This would help both the movement and us personally, and there are a dozen other such tactics we can employ. We could reduce our Netflix binging by five hours a week and spend that time volunteering to phone-bank for Sanders. We can also regularly and respectfully argue for his candidacy on social media. In fact, one of the purposes of this book is to arm Sanders supporters with facts and cogent arguments for precisely this activity. And so on.

Don't just abstractly support the campaign; substantively support it. And allow me to add one more point: the best way to donate is to order a t-shirt or sweatshirt directly from the Bernie Sanders campaign website. Why? Some might know that ordering clothing directly from a campaign is a campaign contribution, meaning that the recipients get money not just for the garment but for the campaign itself (which is why they're so expensive). By buying a garment that you can wear publicly, you are not only supporting the campaign financially, but also publicly when you wear it and show support for how massive this movement is.

In terms of outcome three, there is one simple thing we have to do: even if Clinton has an insurmountable lead later in the primaries, don't stay at home. Go vote for Sanders anyway. This will get him more delegates for the convention and thus give his movement more of a say in how the Democratic Party engages the 2016 general election.

Despite the huge obstacles ahead, there are ways to win, but only if we all get in the game and play it to win it.

CLOSING ARGUMENTS

"[Bernie Sanders] is a long-distance runner with integrity in the struggle for justice for over 50 years. Now is the time for his prophetic voice to be heard across our crisis-ridden country."
– Dr. Cornel West[75]

Bernie Sanders has an outsider's appeal while having all the credentials of a veteran politician. He served four terms as mayor of Burlington, Vermont; he then served eight terms as a member of the House of Representatives; and he is now in his second term as a U.S. Senator. If elected president, he would be one of the most qualified people to hold that position in the country's history. There can be no question of his level of qualification for the job, but some have raised doubts about his electability. Allow me to put those worries to rest once and for all.

The narrative proposed by Clinton supporters is that Sanders has no chance of beating her in the primaries. He has surged in the polls and is now considered a serious threat to her vaunted inevitability. And more importantly, in poll after poll, Sanders beats all of the major Republican candidates by a wider margin than

Clinton does. He also has such a massive support base – and such an incredibly enthusiastic one – that he can mobilize voters on Election Day in a way no other candidate can. It is also worth noting that he has received over 3.5 million individual donations. This fact is noteworthy because it has helped Sanders stay competitive financially with Clinton, even beating her by $5 million in Janurary, and to outpace the Republican candidates in fundraising, but there is another aspect that is generally overlooked. Once people have donated to a campaign, they are literally invested in the success of that campaign and will almost certainly not fall off in support. It is hard to overestimate how important this fact is. When it comes to enthusiastic commitment, Sanders's campaign is outperforming all others by a wide margin, but I argue that this subtler fact about literal investment will lead to unwavering support for the long haul. And, as many commentators have noted, nearly all of Sanders's supporters can donate over and over again, since the average donation is around $30, meaning his donors have not come close to maxing out in terms of legal contribution limits. The loyalty this literal investment in his campaign engenders will lead to many repeat donations, thus making him competitive in the general election and creating an ever-deepening loyalty in his supporters.

I might also add that every time Sanders is attacked by Clinton or one of her surrogates, he raises unprecedented sums of money in a single day. I predict this will not only continue but also increase in the general election. It is this kind of enthusiasm and investment in the political process that our country needs right now and that could easily usher Sanders to a victory in November.

Another charge often leveled at Sanders is that he wouldn't be able to accomplish anything as president. This claim overlooks his many successes in the House of Representatives and in the Senate. He coauthored the Affordable Care Act, which required many compromises, though he always kept his eye on the eventual prize of universal healthcare. He coauthored a major veterans bill with John McCain, thus proving his ability to cross party lines to pass notable legislation. He also has passed more amendments than any other member of Congress. [76] If you add all of this together, you get a portrait of a pragmatic legislator who both understands how Congress works and has been successful there in multiple ways.

Setting aside issues of electability and pragmatism – worries I hope I have assuaged –

there is a larger, more philosophical issue at hand this election cycle. At the core of the Sanders campaign is a fight for the soul of the Democratic Party and the country as a whole. Are we satisfied with the direction of the country is going, where the rich are getting phenomenally richer while the poor and middle-class struggle with basic necessities like housing, healthcare, and college tuition? Are we okay with a campaign finance system that allows billionaires to buy elections? Are we undisturbed by the fact that the United States has more people incarcerated than any other country on Earth? Or are we going to say *enough is enough* and change all of this and more? My fear is that it might already be too late to reverse the course of the nation, but my hope is that people recognize that Bernie Sanders represents the best chance we have of doing so, and that if we get fully behind the Sanders movement, we can elect him president of the United States.

But we must also think of what might happen if he loses the primaries. We can't allow this political enthusiasm to dissipate. Sanders has said repeatedly that his movement is more important than he is individually, and that it's about much more than just electing a single man. I have argued throughout this small book that there has been a building movement that set the foundation for and comprised a large part of the Bernie Sanders Revolution, and I could have reached further back, given the ultimately contiguous nature of history and political progress. We have to think of Bernie Sanders and his supporters as an important portion of this progress, not simply as an end result. I have never believed so fully in a presidential candidate – or a candidate for any office at any level, in fact – and I intend to fight my heart out for Bernie, but I also agree with his own assessment that the larger movement and progress as a whole are more important than a single candidate.

With that said, I'll put aside my consolation-before-the-fact statements, since we absolutely must fight harder than we have ever fought before in our political lives to elect Bernie Sanders, and we have a real chance of winning. We are at a watershed moment in our democracy. If Sanders loses, there will be a clear message sent to other politicians that they cannot run without the heavy help of corporate sponsorship, reducing our leaders to little more than NASCAR drivers in expensive suits. It will also send a message to millions of Americans that our democracy is all but lost to the oligarchic powers-that-be. But if he wins, we could usher in one of the greatest eras of robust democracy and progress our country, and perhaps the world, has ever seen.

National Book Award and Pulitzer Prize winner Norman Mailer wrote: "I am imprisoned with a perception that will settle for nothing less than making a revolution in the consciousness of our time."[77] I have decided that I will settle for nothing less than political revolution and that I am done pretending that the second-rate is anything other than just that. The Sanders movement and all of its myriad parts and members is in the process of effecting just such a revolution in the consciousness of our time, bending the arc of history toward justice, to paraphrase Dr. Martin Luther King Jr.

I beg everyone to join the Bernie Sanders movement, in this election season and beyond. Stoke your enthusiasm to a white-hot heat and refuse to let it cool even after the primary season is over, whether we win or lose. Sanders is the only true progressive in the race, and his movement is the only truly democratic one we're seeing. If millions of us simply donate five dollars and five hours of our time every month from now until November, not only will Sanders win, he will dominate.

Feel the Bern.

ACKNOWLEDGMENTS

First and foremost, I would like to thank Kelly Davio for contacting me about writing a book on Bernie Sanders and for believing I could deliver with such a tight turnaround time. I would also like to thank her for quick and thorough editing on the book. Kelly and I have now worked together at two different presses she's been an editor at, and I can say without the slightest hyperbole that she is one of the best out there. Thanks so much, Kelly. I would also like to thank Todd Swift for accepting the proposal and for his encouragement and professionalism throughout this process. Thanks to Scott Blanchard, Jenn Black, Amanda Caleb, Raul Clement, Renata Fuchs, Matt Hinton, and David Wright for discussing the various thorny patches of the book as I was writing it. And, finally, a huge thanks to one of my political heroes, Matt Gonzalez, for his inspiring presence on the American political scene and for his incredibly kind blurb for the book.

ABOUT THE AUTHOR

Okla Elliott is an assistant professor at Misericordia University in northeast Pennsylvania. He holds a PhD in comparative and world literature from the University of Illinois, a Master of Fine Arts in creative writing from Ohio State University, and a certificate in legal studies from Purdue University. His work has appeared in *Cincinnati Review, Harvard Review, Indiana Review, Prairie Schooner, A Public Space,* and *Subtropics,* and was included as a notable essay in *Best American Essays 2015*. His books include *From the Crooked Timber* (short fiction), *The Cartographer's Ink* (poetry), *The Doors You Mark Are Your Own* (a coauthored novel), and *Blackbirds in September: Selected Shorter Poems of Jürgen Becker* (translation). He is a senior editor at New American Press and the managing editor of the culture and politics website *As It Ought to Be*. For more information about the author, visit www.oklaelliott.net

ENDNOTES

1   Interview with Katie Couric, June 2, 2015.

2   https:berniesanders.com/bernies-announcement/

3   Westfall, Sandra and McAfee Tierney. "Bernie Sanders Does His Own Laundry (and Grocery Shopping): Inside the Family Life of the Down-to-Earth Democratic Candidate. *People*. January 20, 2016.

4   "Getting to Know Jane Sanders, Wife of Bernie." *Bloomberg Politics*, May 25, 2015.

5   Yang, Melissa. "Who Is Levi Sanders, Bernie Sanders' First Son?" *Bustle*, October 12, 2015.

6   *Encyclical Letter* Laudato Si' *of the Holy Father Francis on Care for Our Common Home*, May 24, 2015.

7   Wheeler, Brian. "Is Bernie Sanders the American Jeremy Corbyn?" *BBC News*, January 31, 2016.

8   Birrell, Ian. "Britian's Bernie Sanders May Be Labour's Next Leader." *The Wall Street Journal*, September 4, 2015.

9   "Spin Shift on Bernie: The Escalating Media Assault." *Common Dreams*, January 27, 2016.

10 "Kant, Authority, and the French Revolution," *Journal of the History of Ideas*. University of Pennsylvania Press, 1971.

11 "Contrasting Partisan Perspectives on Campaign 2016." Pew Research Center, October 2, 2015.

12 Borchers, Callum. "Donald Trump Has Gotten More Nightly News Coverage than the Entire Democratic Field." *Washington Post*, December 7, 2015.

13 www.berniesanders.com/democratic-socialism-in-the-united-states/

14 *In These Times*, June 24, 2015.

15 "Vermont's Bernie Sanders Becomes First Socialist Elected to U.S. Senate." *Democracy Now!*, November 8, 2006.

16 "Mobility, Measured." *The Economist*, February 1, 2014.

17 *Washington Post,* January 17, 2016.

18 Neuman, Scott. "States That Raised Minimum Wage See Faster Job Growth, Report Says." NPR. July 19, 2014.

19 Billmoyers.com, June 1, 2015.

20 Billmoyers.com, June 1, 2015.

21 Billmoyers.com, June 1, 2015.

22 Olander, Joseph D. *Isaac Asimov*, Taplinger Publishing Company, 1977.

23 *CBS News*, November 15, 2015.

24 www.berniesanders.com/night-of-the-living-dead-climate-change-style/

25 https://berniesanders.com/issues/money-in-politics/

26 http://www.fec.gov/ans/answers_pac.shtml

27 https://berniesanders.com/issues/money-in-politics/

28 https://berniesanders.com/issues/racial-justice/

29 https://berniesanders.com/issues/racial-justice/

30 https://berniesanders.com/issues/racial-justice/

31 Bennett, John. "Gallup Poll: 58 percent of Americans now Support Marijuana Legalization." *The Daily Caller*, October 21, 2015.

32 "Sanders the Socialist Sure Gets it Right on Big Banks." *Chicago Sun-Times*, May 1, 2015.

33 *The Hill*, January 11, 2016.

34 Kilgore, Samantha. "170 Top Economists 'Feel the Bern,' Endorse Bernie Sanders' Wall Street Reform Plan. *Inquistr*. January 15, 2016.

35 www.sanders.senate.gov

36 www.sanders.senate.gov

37 Kasperkevic, Jana, and Allen, Katie. "Global Markets Fall after U.S. Jobs Report Raises Prospect of Interest Rate Hike." *The Guardian*. February 5, 2016.

38 Landers, Ann. "Things You Always Wanted to Know About Belly Buttons." *The Dispatch*, October 4, 1975.

39 https://berniesanders.com/issues/its-time-to-make-college-tuition-free-and-debt-free/

40 Warren, Elizabeth. "One Way to Rebuild Our Institutions." *The New York Times*. January 29, 2016.

41 http://www.aft.org/election2016/candidate-questionnaire-bernie-sanders

42 http://www.fairtest.org/polls-teachers-reject-nclb

43 http://www.gallup.com/poll/156800/no-child-left-behind-rated-negatively-positively.aspx

44 http://www.aft.org/election2016/candidate-questionnaire-bernie-sanders

45 "Dalai Lama says strong action on climate change is a human responsibility." *The Guardian*, October 20, 2015.

46 http://scorecard.lcv.org/moc/bernie-sanders

47 "Is Bernie Sanders the Best Candidate on Climate Change?" *Mother Jones*, May 14, 2015.

48 Linney, Grant. "The Paris Climate Agreement: Success that Teeters on Failure." *The Hamilton Spectator*. January 5, 2016.

49 Simon, Roger. "Obama Beats Hillary over the Head with Iraq." *Salon.com*, January 31, 2008.

50 www.sanders.senate.gov

51 www.sanders.senate.gov

52 Hensch, Mark. "Sanders Sees 'Consensus for Serious Gun Control'." *The Hill*. October 2, 2015.

53 "Guns in the U.S.: the Statistics behind the Violence." *BBC News*. January 5, 2016.

54 "Guns in the U.S.: the Statistics behind the Violence." *BBC News*. January 5, 2016.

55 Chasmar, Jessica. "Bernie Sanders: '99.9 Percent' of Gun Owners Obey the Law." *The Washington Times*. July 7, 2015.

56 Rosenfeld, Steven. "Bernie Sanders Critics Misfire: the Vermont Senator's Gun Record Is Better than It Looks." *Salon*. October 10, 2015.

57 Edelman, Adam. "Vast Majority of Americans Favor Tougher Gun Control." *NY Daily News*. December 3, 2015.

58 Klein, Naomi. *The Shock Doctrine: The Rise of Disaster Capitalism*. New York: Henry Holt, 2007.

59 Sanders, Bernie. *Congressional Record* 156:163, December 10, 2010.

60 http://www.apta.com/resources/reportsandpublications/ Documents/economic_impact_of_public_transportation_ investment.pdf

61 http://www.apta.com/mediacenter/pressreleases/2013/ Pages/130530_Transit-Savings.aspx

62 "D.C. Has Worst Traffic in the U.S., Study Says." NBC Washington. August 26, 2015.

63 Ramazzina, Yoli. "Susan Sarandon Feels the Bern." *Elephant Journal*, January 7, 2016.

64 Murphy, Tim. "The Time Gloria Steinem Made Bernie Sanders an 'Honorary Woman.'" *Mother Jones*, January 20, 2016.

65 Richardson, Bradford. "Sanders Campaign Says it Has More Women Donors than Clinton." *The Hill*, November 25, 2015.

66 Brodsky, Rachel. "Berning for You: If Nothing Else, Sanders Has Won Over Williamsburg." *SPIN*, January 7, 2016.

67 https://votesmart.org/candidate/evaluations/27110/bernie-sanders#.Vq5rkdC18zU

68 Frizell, Sam. "How Bernie Sanders Evolved on Gay Marriage." *TIME*, October 28, 2015.

69 Dimock, Chase. "Bernie Sanders' Gay Pride Parade Proclamation and the History of LGBT Advocacy." *As It Ought to Be*, January 28, 2016.

70 LoGiurato, Brett. "Bernie sanders Just Melted Away 30-Point Hillary Clinton Lead in a new Poll." *Business Insider*. February 5, 2016.

71 http://www.bls.gov/opub/reports/cps/characteristics-of-minimum-wage-workers-2014.pdf

72 Mailer, Norman. *The Time of Our Time*. Random House, 1998.

73 Barkan, Ross. "What's a Superdelegate Anyway?" *Observer*. December 28, 2015.

74 Barkan, Ross. "What's a Superdelegate Anyway?" *Observer*. December 28, 2015.

75 https://www.facebook.com/drcornelwest/posts/10155953989390111 [accessed 1/30/2016]

76 Jilani, Zaid. "Bernie Gets It Done." *Alternet*, October 17, 2015.

77 Mailer, Norman. *The Time of Our Time*. Random House, 1998.

◯◯ **EYEWEAR** PUBLISHING

we are an independent press
based in London, England.
Emphasis is on excellent new
work, in poetry and prose. Our
range is international and our
aim is true. Look into some of the
most stylish books around today.

SQUINT BOOKS
W STEPHEN GILBERT JEREMY CORBYN – ACCIDENTAL HERO
OKLA ELLIOTT BERNIE SANDERS – THE ESSENTIAL GUIDE
AMY MACKELDEN ADELE – THE OTHER SIDE

EYEWEAR PROSE
SUMIA SUKKAR THE BOY FROM ALEPPO WHO PAINTED THE WAR
ALFRED CORN MIRANDA'S BOOK

EYEWEAR LITERARY CRITICISM
MARK FORD THIS DIALOGUE OF ONE - WINNER OF THE 2015 PEGASUS AWARD
FOR POETRY CRITICISM FROM THE POETRY FOUNDATION (CHICAGO, USA).

EYEWEAR POETRY
MORE THAN 30 TITLES

SEE **WWW.EYEWEARPUBLISHING.COM**